Helpfulness

Kimberley Jane Pryor

 **Marshall Cavendish**
Benchmark
New York

Other Marshall Cavendish Offices: Marshall Cavendish International (Asia) Private Limited, 1 New Industrial Road, Singapore 536196 • Marshall Cavendish International (Thailand) Co Ltd. 253 Asoke, 12th Flr, Sukhumvit 21 Road, Klongtoey Nua, Wattana, Bangkok 10110, Thailand • Marshall Cavendish (Malaysia) Sdn Bhd, Times Subang, Lot 46, Subang Hi-Tech Industrial Park, Batu Tiga, 40000 Shah Alam, Selangor Darul Ehsan, Malaysia

Marshall Cavendish is a trademark of Times Publishing Limited

All websites were available and accurate when this book was sent to press.

Library of Congress Cataloging-in-Publication Data

Pryor, Kimberley Jane.
  Helpfulness / Kimberley Jane Pryor.
     p. cm. — (Values)
  Includes index.
  Summary: "Discusses what values are, why being helpful is a worthwhile value and how to be helpful"—Provided by publisher.
  ISBN 978-1-60870-144-5
  1. Helping behavior—Juvenile literature. 2. Children—Conduct of life—Juvenile literature. I. Title.
  BF637.H4P79 2011
  179'.9—dc22

                                        2009042682

First published in 2010 by
MACMILLAN EDUCATION AUSTRALIA PTY LTD
15–19 Claremont Street, South Yarra 3141

Visit our website at www.macmillan.com.au or go directly to www.macmillanlibrary.com.au

Associated companies and representatives throughout the world.

Copyright © Kimberley Jane Pryor 2010

Managing Editor: Vanessa Lanaway
Editor: Helena Newton
Proofreader: Kirstie Innes-Will
Designer: Kerri Wilson
Page layout: Pier Vido
Photo researcher: Sarah Johnson (management: Debbie Gallagher)
Production Controller: Vanessa Johnson

Printed in China

Acknowledgments
The author and the publisher are grateful to the following for permission to reproduce copyright material:

Front cover photograph: Children playing with brother pushing sister in swing, Maike Jessen/Photolibrary

Photos courtesy of:
Getty Images, **26**; Paul Bailey/Getty Images, **19**; Paul Burns/Getty Images, **25**; Lauren Burke/Getty Images, **16**; Peter Dazeley/Getty Images, **24**; Jody Faussett/Getty Images, **8**; Paul Harris/Getty Images, **30**; Sean Justice/Getty Images, **11**; Amanda Marsalis/Getty Images, **17**; Robert Nicholas/Getty Images, **21**; Lori Adamski Peek/Getty Images, **28**; Stephen Swain Photography/Getty Images, **9**; STOCK4B/Getty Images, **15**; Stephanie Wolfsteiner/Getty Images, **5**; © Ziva Kirn/iStockphoto, **4**; © Nina Shannon/iStockphoto, **12**; Jupiter Unlimited, **3**, **7**; Foodpix/Photolibrary, **20**; Imagesource/Photolibrary, **27**; Maike Jessen/Photolibrary, **1**, **18**; Jutta Klee/Photolibrary, **14**; Peter Mason/Photolibrary, **10**; Jochen Sand/Photolibrary, **22**; © AVAVA/Shutterstock, **6**; © michaeljung/Shutterstock, **13**; Stockxpert, **23**, **29**.

While every care has been taken to trace and acknowledge copyright, the publisher tenders their apologies for any accidental infringement where copyright has proved untraceable. Where the attempt has been unsuccessful, the publisher welcomes information that would redress the situation.

For Nick, Ashley, and Thomas

135642

Contents

When a word is printed in **bold**, you can look up its meaning in the Glossary on page 31.

Values

Values are the things you believe in. They guide the way:

- you think
- you speak
- you **behave**

Values help you to behave well when you are skiing.

Values help you to decide what is right and what is wrong. They also help you to live your life in a **meaningful** way.

Values help you to follow the rules when you have a hula hoop contest.

Helpfulness

Helpfulness is giving **assistance** to others when they need it. It is giving the right kind of assistance at the right time.

It is helpful to hold a model car steady while a friend fixes it.

Helpfulness is also noticing what needs to be done, and doing it without being asked. It is doing these jobs as well as you can.

Helpful people notice when flowers need to be watered, and they water them.

Helpful People

Helpful people join in when others are working. If they are unsure of what needs to be done, they ask, "How can I help?"

It can be fun to wash a car when several family members help.

Helpful people also look for ways to be useful. They enjoy making life easier for their family, friends, and neighbors.

Weeding a community vegetable garden is very helpful.

Being Helpful to Family

Helpful people give assistance to family members. They help younger family members to do things they cannot do by themselves. They also help them to reach things they cannot reach.

A younger family member may need help to climb into a tree house.

It is helpful to visit family members who are ill. You can help them feel better by telling them interesting stories. You can also listen to them.

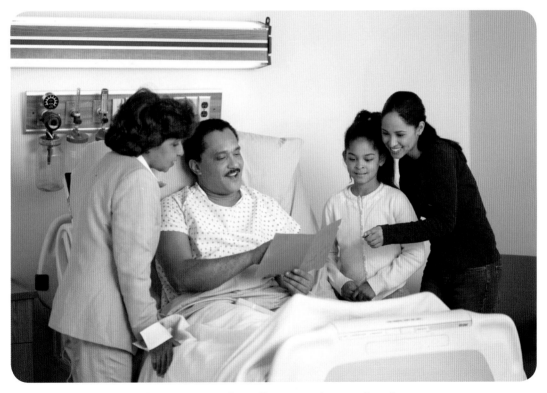

It is helpful to cheer up a family member who has to stay in the hospital.

Being Helpful to Friends

Helpful people give assistance to their friends.
They know that some things are difficult to do alone.

It is helpful to paint your friend's fingernails
before a special event.

Friends help each other to learn new information and practice new **skills**. They sometimes do homework together or practice sports together.

Friends sometimes help each other by practicing their soccer skills together.

Being Helpful to Neighbors

Helpful people get to know their neighbors. They offer to help their neighbors during **emergencies**. They also ask their neighbors for help when they need it.

It is helpful to hang laundry up to dry for a neighbor who is sick.

You can make your neighborhood a better place by helping people in need. You could help by serving meals to homeless people or by reading to people who cannot see well.

Some older people need help to read the small print in newspapers.

Ways To Be Helpful

There are many different ways to be helpful to your family, friends, and neighbors. Helping younger people and pets is a good way to start.

You can help a younger family member tie her shoelaces.

You can also offer to help busy people. Teaching others and listening to others are good ways to be helpful, too.

Listening to older family members shows that you love them and value their ideas.

Helping Younger People and Pets

You can help younger people and pets do things they cannot do for themselves. Younger people often need help with activities they have not learned to do yet.

A younger family member may need help to use a swing.

Pets need help to stay happy and healthy. They need food and clean water every day. They also need places to exercise and places to rest.

It is helpful to show your pet hamster where its food is.

Helping Busy People

You can help busy people by doing things they do not have time to do. A person doing one important job may not have time to do another important job.

It is helpful to set the table if a family member is busy making dinner.

Family members may sometimes be busy with work or school projects. They may not have time to do jobs around the home. They may need extra help until they finish their projects.

Washing the dishes while other family members are working on a project is helpful.

Making Life Easier

Making life easier is also a way to be helpful. Many families work together to do jobs around the house and in the garden. This helps them to get everything done.

Food shopping can be done more quickly if everyone helps.

Helpful people put things away after using them. They know that keeping things in the right place makes life easier.

Helpful people put pencils back in their container after using them.

Teaching Others

Teaching others is a helpful thing to do.
Helpful people enjoy teaching others new skills.

If you teach your
friend a song,
you can have fun
singing together.

You can teach others by **explaining** what to do or how to do it. You can also show others what to do or how to do it.

Showing a family member how to use a webcam is very helpful.

Listening to Others

Listening to others can be very helpful. Helpful people listen carefully to friends who feel sad. They do not **interrupt** or try to give unwanted **advice**.

Friends who feel sad often need others to listen to them.

Listening to others shows that you care about their feelings and needs. It can help people understand their feelings, and what to do about them.

Listening to new friends can help you to understand their point of view.

Helping Our World

Helping our world is very important. Helping animals to **survive** is one way to help our world. Planting trees and shrubs helps to provide food and homes for animals.

Leafy plants provide shelter for butterflies.

Reusing is another way to help our world. Taking your lunch to school in a lunch box is one way to reuse. The same lunch box can be used for many years.

Using a lunch box instead of a paper bag helps our world.

Personal Set of Values

There are many different values. Everyone has a personal set of values. This set of values guides people in big and little ways in their daily lives.

A tour guide helps people learn about new places.

Glossary

advice   An idea or ideas about what you think someone should do.

assistance   A helping hand.

behave   Act in a certain way.

emergencies   Serious, unwanted things that happen when you do not expect them to, and that need to have something done about them at once.

explaining   Making something easy for people to understand.

interrupt   Break in or cut someone off by talking when they are talking.

meaningful   Important or valuable.

skills   Abilities that help you to do activities or jobs well.

survive   Stay alive.

Index